The Horseshoe Crab

The Horseshoe Crab

By Nancy Day

DILLON PRESS
New York

Maxwell Macmillan Canada
Toronto

Maxwell Macmillan International
New York   Oxford   Singapore   Sydney

To my parents, Robert and Betty Day, and my husband,
Joe Sakaduski, for their support and encouragement.

Acknowledgments

My sincerest gratitude goes to Carl N. Shuster, Jr., Ph.D., for generously donating
his time, expert advice, drawings, and photographs. Special thanks to Robert B.
Barlow, Jr., Ph.D., for reviewing the manuscript and giving valuable technical
assistance. I would also like to thank Benjie Lynn Swan of Finn-Tech Industries,
Inc., Carla Dietze, Linda Kelly-Hassett, and Polly Chandler for reviewing the
manuscript.

Photo Credits

Front Cover by Jim White; Back Cover by Nancy Day
Interior: Nancy Day, frontispiece, title page, 16, 25, 26, 52; Jim White, 8, 28, 30, 31;
Dr. Peter Weidner, 10; Dr. Thomas J. Novitsky, 12, 36, 42, 48; John G. Shuster, 14;
Board of Agriculture, Delaware State Archives, 19; Dr. Carl N. Shuster, 23, 41;
Franklin J. Viola, 34, 38; Dr. Frederick C. Pearson, 40; Dr. Robert B. Barlow, Jr., 44

Library of Congress Cataloging-in-Publication Data

Day, Nancy.
    The horseshoe crab / by Nancy Day. — 1st ed.
    p.   cm.
    Includes index.
    Summary: Describes the physical characteristics, habits, and life cycle of this
ancient arthropod and discusses its importance to medical research.
    ISBN 0-87518-545-2
    1. Limulus polyphemus—Juvenile literature. 2. Limulus polyphemus—Re-
search—Juvenile literature. 3. Limulus test—Juvenile literature. [1. Horseshoe
crabs.] I. Title. II Series.
QL447.7.D38 1992   595.3'92—dc20   92-9772

Maxwell Macmillan Canada, Inc.
1200 Eglinton Avenue East
Suite 200
Don Mills, Ontario M3C 3N1

Dillon Press
Macmillan Publishing Company
866 Third Avenue
New York, NY 10022

Macmillan Publishing Company is part of the Maxwell Communication Group of
Companies.

First edition

Printed in the United States of America

10   9   8   7   6   5   4   3   2   1

Contents

Facts about the Horseshoe Crab

Scientific Name: *Limulus polyphemus*

Description (of the adult animal):

Length: Up to 24 inches (60 centimeters), including tail; females are larger than males

Weight: Up to 10 pounds (4.5 kilograms)

Physical Features: A divided body that includes a large, helmet-shaped front, a middle section, and a long, spikelike tail; 5 pairs of legs, 10 eyes, and blue blood

Color: Dark olive-green/brown

Distinctive Habits: Turns itself over by sticking its tail in the sand and flipping over; sometimes swims upside down, especially during the larval stage; growth occurs through molting—the old shell is discarded and replaced by a larger new shell

Food: Small or soft-shelled clams, sea worms

Reproductive Cycle: Females lay eggs in late May or early June on high tides, usually during the full moon or new moon; males latch onto the females' backs, fertilizing the eggs as they are laid in sand nests on the beach or near the water's edge

Life Span: 15 to 20 years

Range: Three species of horseshoe crabs live in limited numbers along the coasts of India, Japan, and Indonesia; the fourth species, *Limulus polyphemus*, is found along the East Coast of North America, between Maine and the Yucatán Peninsula

Habitat: Tidewater areas—the shallow saltwater bays and inlets along the ocean shore—and the continental shelf

The areas in orange show the range of *Limulus polyphemus*.

Horseshoe crabs have interested people for thousands of years. This junior naturalist is studying their habits as part of a program sponsored by the Delaware Nature Society.

Chapter 1

A Living Fossil

It is a warm day in North America. But, then, every day is warm. The equator runs right across where the United States one day will be. The North Pole is somewhere near Japan. The Atlantic Ocean is enclosed by land. Animals walk from North America to Europe and never even get their feet wet. The Rocky Mountains have not yet formed. There are no birds. The Great Ice Age is still over 200 million years in the future. Dinosaurs roam the land. Yet one creature is already ancient —over 100 million years old—the horseshoe crab.

   The horseshoe crab you find on the beach today looks almost exactly the same as the ones that lived with the dinosaurs. Its ancestors go back over 500 million years. The **evolutionary*** process that turned some reptiles into birds in just 50 million years left

*Words in **bold type** are explained in the glossary at the end of this book.

This fossil of a horseshoe crab is over 150 million years old. Yet when a living horseshoe crab is placed on top, it's an almost perfect match.

horseshoe crabs almost untouched for more than 300 million years. That's why some people call them **living fossils**.

Many people walk by horseshoe crabs on the beach without giving them a second look. Yet these curious creatures hold amazing secrets. Only in the last 50 years or so have scientists begun to discover some of these secrets. They've learned that horseshoe crabs have some unique features that make them very important to people.

The crab's unusual eyes have helped researchers understand eyesight. The special design of its heart has helped scientists learn more about how our own hearts work. Horseshoe crab shells have been used to make bandages that help wounds heal faster. But one of the horseshoe crab's most important secrets is in its blood.

A Real Blue Blood

The difference between human blood and the blood of a horseshoe crab can be seen in a single glance:

The horseshoe crab's blue blood is of great interest to scientists.

When exposed to air, horseshoe crab blood is bright blue! Besides being unusual in color, the blood has unusual properties. Drug manufacturers use horseshoe crab blood in a test to make sure drugs are pure enough to be injected into the human body. The test can also detect unusual infections in people and animals. Because of its many scientific uses, and the high cost of processing it, horseshoe crab blood is quite valuable. Just one quart of processed blood can be worth as much as $15,000.

Horseshoe crabs are important to birds as well as people. Each year the crabs lay billions of eggs on beaches along the East Coast of the United States. The greatest number are laid along the Delaware Bay. There they provide a crucial feeding stop for millions of shorebirds on their way to nesting areas near the Arctic Circle.

Horseshoe crabs are as old as time and yet are important to modern medicine. By studying these remarkable creatures, scientists are discovering the keys to long-term survival. Horseshoe crabs are simple in some ways and very complex in others. For these and many other reasons, they have become the most studied marine animal in the world.

The "Horseshoe Crab Man"

As a college student in the mid-1940s, Carl Shuster had been interested in chickens and turkeys. Then a professor handed him a jar of horseshoe crab eggs and said, "Study these." Curious about the strange creatures, Carl followed his professor's advice and studied them for several years. Yet even after finishing school and getting an advanced degree, he hadn't seen horseshoe crabs in the wild. He had studied preserved or "pickled" specimens, never the living animal.

One day in 1948 he got to see the real thing. He

Dr. Carl N. Shuster, Jr., has been studying horseshoe crabs for almost 50 years. This photograph, taken in 1951, shows him holding a very large female crab.

and his professor walked out onto a beach north of Cape May, New Jersey, during the horseshoe crab's mating period. As he walked toward the water through a pre-dawn mist, he saw a "mystical, magical sight."

Dozens of horseshoe crabs were scrambling toward shore just as others like them had done every year for millions of years.

"For a moment, I felt as if I had stepped out of modern day into prehistoric times," Carl said. "That was really exciting." Since that day, he has been fascinated by these odd animals. Now he has the world's largest collection of information on horseshoe crabs and is considered the leading expert on them. He has even eaten the meat of the horseshoe crab. (He reports that there's not much of it—considering the size of the animal—and that it doesn't taste as good as the meat of a blue crab.)

Dr. Shuster and other scientists are still working to solve the many mysteries about horseshoe crabs. How far do they travel? How long can they live? Why did they survive when the dinosaurs became **extinct** and died out? What can we learn from their success? Although nearly 50 years have gone by, Dr. Shuster is still following his professor's advice to study the horseshoe crab.

Although people are sometimes hesitant to touch horseshoe crabs, they are basically harmless.

Chapter 2

The Crab That's Not a Crab

Horseshoe crabs and their relatives were among the most common animals on earth before the dinosaurs appeared. The crabs lived in the shallow seas where the continents of Europe and North America are now. As the continents shifted, horseshoe crabs followed the changing shorelines. Now there are only four **species**, or kinds, of horseshoe crabs left. Three of them are found only around India, Japan, and Indonesia, and their populations are small. The Japanese horseshoe crab has even become **endangered**, or in danger of dying out.

The species that is largest in number, *Limulus polyphemus*, lives along the East Coast of North America, between Maine and the Yucatán Peninsula.

The total adult population of these horseshoe crabs may be as high as ten million. About nine million live in the waters between Long Island in New York State and Cape Hatteras in North Carolina. Even within that small area, some places have few, if any, horseshoe crabs. Other places, such as the Delaware Bay, are home to huge numbers of crabs.

Partner or Pest?

Native Americans were familiar with the horseshoe crab and found many uses for it. Its tail made a good sharp spear tip. Its meat could be eaten. It made good bait for fishing. And its shell was useful, especially for bailing out wet canoes. Native Americans were also the first to discover that horseshoe crabs make an excellent fertilizer, or plant food.

Fishermen consider horseshoe crabs pests because they get caught in fishing nets and are hard to untangle. This was an even bigger problem in the 1800s, when the crab population was much larger. Then someone came up with the idea of

During the 1920s, when this photograph was taken, horseshoe crabs were still being harvested to use as fertilizer.

"harvesting" the crabs. Every year people collected the crabs as they came ashore to reproduce. They stacked them in huge piles and left them to dry in the sun. Later, they took the dried crabs to factories, where they were ground up for fertilizer. By the 1870s, more than four million crabs were being killed each year. Some towns on Cape Cod in Massachusetts put a bounty on horseshoe crabs. The town of Orleans, for example, paid 20 cents for each male and

50 cents for each female crab that was killed.

The horseshoe crab population dropped to dangerously low levels. By the 1960s, the annual harvest of adult horseshoe crabs in the Delaware Bay area was estimated at under 50,000. Commercial harvesting stopped because there were too few crabs to pay for the time spent collecting them.

By 1977, the number of adult crabs in the Delaware Bay had increased to about 270,000. The horseshoe crab population had begun to come back. Fortunately, by this time the value of the crabs was well known and scientists were able to take steps to protect them.

The Spider's Cousin

The horseshoe crab is actually not a crab at all. It belongs to a large group of animals called **arthropods**. They include insects, spiders, scorpions, and ticks. True crabs, such as the blue crab, are also part of this group but are only distant relatives of the horseshoe crab.

Like other arthropods, the horseshoe crab is an **invertebrate**—an animal with no backbone—and has an **exoskeleton**—a skeleton on the outside of its body. While true crabs have only one pair of claws, horseshoe crabs have more. Also, true crabs have **antennae**, or feelers, on their heads; horseshoe crabs do not. Another thing that makes horseshoe crabs different from true crabs is that they don't have jaws. The horseshoe crab "chews" its food by rubbing it between its shoulders (the bases of its legs). Then it pushes the broken-down food into its mouth, which is located between its legs. So, although the horseshoe crab you see on the beach looks like a crab, it is actually more closely related to a spider.

Horseshoe crabs grow to about 2 feet (60 centimeters) in length, including their tails. They can weigh up to 10 pounds (4.5 kilograms). The females are larger than the males. Horseshoe crabs seem to live about 15 to 20 years. They crawl along the ocean bottom and in shallow bays, eating small or soft-shelled clams and sea worms. In turn, horseshoe crabs are sometimes eaten by fish, sharks, turtles, and birds.

The horseshoe crab's shell is its main protection. A brownish covering shields its entire body. It is very hard on top and around the rim of the shell, but it is soft and leathery in other places. This material, called **chitin**, is also found in shrimp and crab shells. It is similar to the substance in animal hooves, horns, and claws.

The body of the horseshoe crab is divided into three sections: the helmet-shaped front, the middle section, and the spikelike tail. Attached to the underside of the front section are five pairs of legs. The horseshoe crab uses its legs for walking, swimming, and eating. The legs have pincers, or claws, on the ends to help the crab hold food. In addition, the crab has an extra pair of small pincers that grab and push food toward the legs.

When the male crab becomes an adult, the first pair of legs changes into claspers that are used for holding on to the female during mating. By looking

Adult male *Limulus polyphemus* from Delaware Bay

Top **Underside**

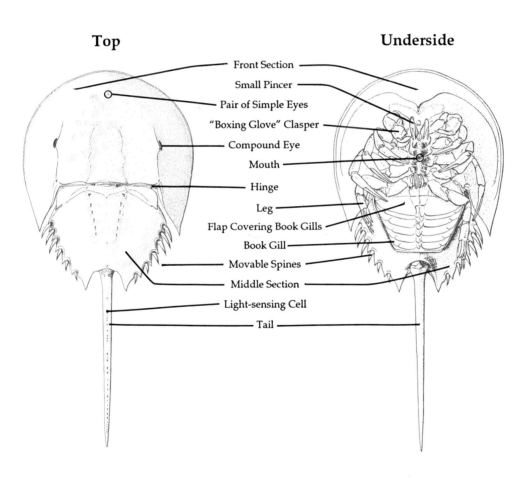

Front Section

Small Pincer

Pair of Simple Eyes

"Boxing Glove" Clasper

Compound Eye

Mouth

Hinge

Leg

Flap Covering Book Gills

Book Gill

Movable Spines

Middle Section

Light-sensing Cell

Tail

23

for these "boxing glove"-shaped claspers, you can tell a male horseshoe crab from a female.

The crab's belly, or middle section, is attached to the front section by a large hinge. On the underside is a flap that covers five pairs of **gills**. Each gill of an adult crab contains a stack of over 100 paper-thin, oval-shaped leaves. Rhythmic beating of the flap and gills forces water between the leaves, ruffling them like the pages of a book. Oxygen passes through the leaves into the crab's blood. This is how a horseshoe crab "breathes."

Although it looks like a stinger, the horseshoe crab's sharp tail is not poisonous. It's not even dangerous, unless you happen to step on it in bare feet! It is very useful to the crab, however. Waves at the water's edge can turn a crab upside down. If it remains upside down on the beach, its gills will dry out and the crab will die. To turn over, the crab sticks its tail into the sand. Then it kicks its legs and arches its body, bending at the hinge. This action makes it flip over. The crab's tail also contains a set of light

This crab is trying to turn itself right side up with its tail.

sensors—a primitive kind of eye.

The heart of the adult horseshoe crab is about the size and shape of a long, thin link of breakfast sausage. Its design is of great interest to scientists. The nerve that connects the heart to the brain lies on the outside of the heart, where it can be easily examined. Some of the important facts about our own hearts have been learned by studying the heart of the horseshoe crab.

If you gently turn a horseshoe crab upside down, you will be able to see many of its anatomical features.

The relationship between horseshoe crabs and shorebirds is a long and important one. Without horseshoe crab eggs as a source of food, many birds would never reach their nesting areas in northern Canada in time to reproduce.

Chapter 3

Life Along the Beach

Horseshoe crabs live in tidewater areas—shallow saltwater bays and inlets. In some areas, they may travel to the floor of the **continental shelf**, the shallow underwater plain that borders continents. They need to be able to reach sandy beaches, where they can lay their eggs, protected from the heavy surges of the ocean waves.

During the colder months, they burrow into the ocean bottom. Horseshoe crabs are very sensitive to changes in temperature. Even a five-degree drop will cause them to dig themselves into the sand for warmth. Using the fronts of their shells to push the sand out of the way, they dig deeper and deeper. Like small bulldozers, they push forward using their legs and the action of their hinged bodies.

The height of the horseshoe crab's egg-laying usually occurs at night. At the night high tide during the mating period, thousands of crabs crowd the water's edge.

Burrowing into the sand also protects the crab from **predators**—animals that would eat them. The horseshoe crab has few natural enemies, but when their undersides are exposed, fish and birds can rip them open.

In the spring, horseshoe crabs dig out and begin to walk along the ocean floor. No one knows for sure how they know when to come ashore to reproduce. Perhaps some combination of water temperature and day length tells them. Tide activity also gives them timing clues. Another mystery is how they find their way to the beach. It may be a magnetic sense, like the force that pulls the compass needle.

A Seaside Omelet

If you were to stroll along the shores of the Delaware Bay during a high tide in late May or early June, you

Each female horseshoe crab lays thousands of small greenish eggs.

might have a hard time even taking a step. As many as 20,000 crabs crowd a single mile of beach. Once a year, horseshoe crabs come ashore or to the water's edge to lay their eggs. At the same time, over a million shorebirds arrive from as far away as South America. The birds fly more than 2,000 miles (3,200 kilometers), arriving just in time to feast on the horseshoe crab eggs.

The Delaware Bay is a crucial feeding stop for

these shorebirds on their way to northern Canada to lay eggs of their own. The birds must go far north, mate, make their nests, lay their eggs, hatch their young, and then head south before the Arctic cold front starts coming in by mid-August. They depend upon the horseshoe crab egg feast to provide enough energy to get them to their nesting areas in time. At least 11 types of shorebirds, three kinds of gulls, cowbirds, grackles, mourning doves, house finches, starlings, house sparrows, and even pigeons feed upon the eggs. In just three weeks, many of the birds will double their weight. J. P. "Pete" Myers, former chief scientist at the National Audubon Society, figured out that he would have to eat 197 jars of peanut butter in addition to his usual meals to do the same thing!

Concerns for the Future

So many birds depend upon the horseshoe crab eggs that many people are concerned for the birds' survival. If for some reason the horseshoe crabs were unable to lay their eggs on the shores of the Delaware Bay, or if the number of eggs dropped drastically, the birds would lose an essential source of food. Without enough food, the birds might not make it to their own egg-laying areas. Whole species of birds could be affected.

Other animals eat horseshoe crab eggs, too. Raccoons and other small mammals eat eggs lying on the beach. Small fish, particularly minnows and young weakfish, eat horseshoe crab eggs in the water. All of the animals that feed on horseshoe crab eggs would suffer if the supply were suddenly cut off.

Scientists are concerned about the future of horseshoe crabs as well. The crabs need shallow bays for reproduction. Many of these bays are becoming polluted. Valuable nesting areas are being gobbled up by seaside development. Fishermen still use horseshoe crabs for eel bait, although laws are being passed to limit this practice. There is fear that while the horseshoe crab has witnessed much of the history of this planet, it will not survive the next hundred years.

Dr. Shuster (right) and others tag horseshoe crabs so that the crabs' movements can be followed.

In an attempt to learn more about the habits of the crabs—and thus insure their survival—scientists tag them. They capture crabs and attach identification tags to their shells. Then they record where and when each crab is released. The crab's size and condition are also recorded. When tagged crabs are found, scientists gain important information about their activities. If you find a tagged crab, write down the tag number, the date, where you found it, and the phone number printed on the tag. If the crab is alive, you should release it, still tagged, and report the information by calling the phone number on the tag.

During the mating period, the male uses his claspers to hang on to the female. As she lays the eggs in sand nests, he fertilizes them.

36

Chapter 4

A Horseshoe Crab Is Born

It is a quiet night late in May on the Delaware Bay. A full moon exerts its pull on the waters, creating high tide. As if answering some unknown call, the crabs come ashore by the hundreds of thousands. The male uses its claspers to hold on to the female's back. She drags him along as she lays her eggs in the several different nests she makes on the beach, usually near the edge of the water. The female crab digs holes in the beach about 6 inches (15 centimeters) deep to make the nests. She usually lays thousands of eggs— sometimes as many as 100,000.

As the male is dragged into the nest, he releases **sperm**, the cells that **fertilize** the eggs. The sperm washes over the eggs. Only eggs that are fertilized can develop into **embryos** and eventually become new crabs.

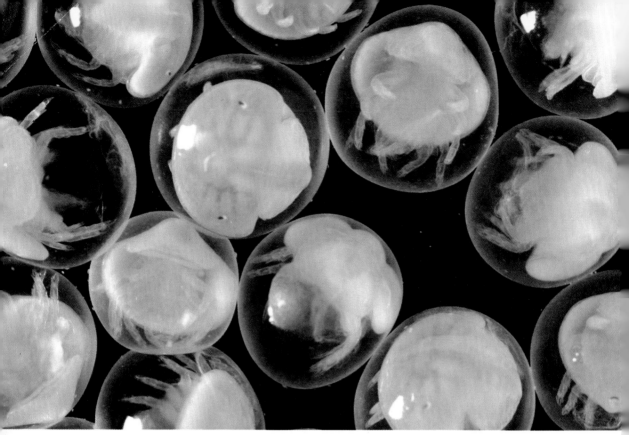

Horseshoe crab embryos can be clearly seen through the fluid-filled sacs that balloon out from the fertilized eggs.

Out of the Nest, into the Sea

A fertilized horseshoe crab egg lies in its sand nest. It is green, soft, and sticky. Thousands of eggs just like it crowd the nest. Inside the egg, the embryo begins to grow. After a few days, the outer coating of the egg begins to split. A clear, fluid-filled sac containing the embryo balloons out. The embryo is weighted so that it floats upside down in the sac. The embryo sheds its shell, or **molts**, several times as it gets bigger.

After three weeks, the embryo is developed enough to be called a **larva** and is ready to hatch. The full-moon tide, the highest since the eggs were laid, is coming. The larva seems to sense the rising tide and kicks its way out of the egg sac. With the other larvae in the nest, it begins to dig its way toward the surface of the sand. Water washes over the larva and it floats out into the sea. A new horseshoe crab has been "born."

At this stage, the larvae are often called **trilobite** larvae because they resemble animals, called trilobites, that lived hundreds of millions of years ago. The larva's digestive tract, the system needed to eat and use food, is not yet fully formed. A portion of the egg's yolk remains inside the larva and provides food while it develops to the next stage. At that time, the digestive tract is complete.

Up until now, the larva has spent its life upside down. Its tail is only a stub. Later, when its tail is larger and it is a fully formed crab, it will learn to turn itself right side up. The larva swims upward and then

Newly hatched larvae resemble trilobites, ancient sea animals. At this early stage, the horseshoe crab's tail is only a stub.

drifts down, over and over again. After about six days, it molts for the first time since it left the egg sac. Then it settles to the bottom. Although it will keep its ability to swim, it is mainly a creature of the ocean bottom from now on.

By late fall, three to four months after entering its larval stage, the crab may have molted five times. Yet it is still less than an inch (2½ centimeters) wide. It will spend the next ten years or so, until it reaches adulthood, searching for food and growing bigger. During this period, the crab will change shells ten or more times.

Before molting, the crab forms a new skin beneath its old shell. This skin has pleats, like a folded umbrella, which allow the animal to expand in size. The shell splits around the edge of the front of the

When the crab molts, it crawls out of its old shell (right). Its new shell begins to harden when it comes into contact with seawater.

crab. The crab crawls out, the pleats in its new skin unfolding as the animal swells by taking in water. For a very young crab, this process may take less than an hour. But for an older, larger crab, it may take as long as 24 hours. Older crabs dig into the sandy bottom while molting, protecting themselves from predators that could easily bite through the soft new shell.

During the first two or three years, the crab may molt several times. From then on, it usually will molt only once a year until it reaches maturity in nine to eleven years. At that time, the crab is an adult—fully grown and able to reproduce.

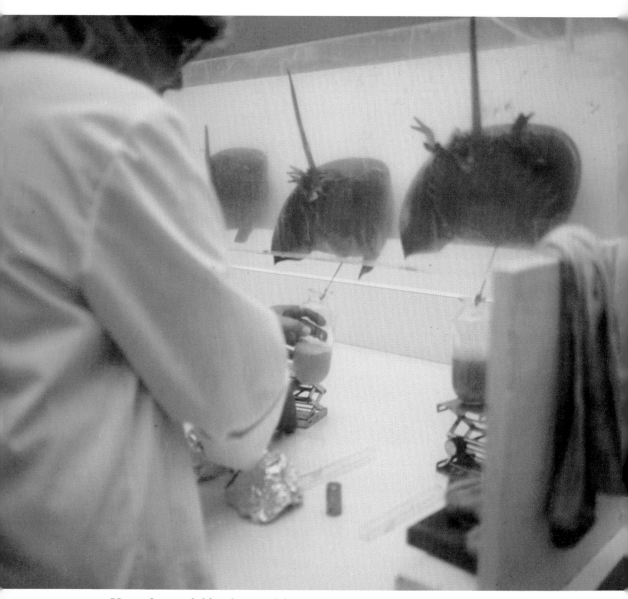

Horseshoe crab blood is used for medical and research purposes. Crabs are returned to the sea after making their "donation."

Chapter 5

At the Forefront of Modern Medicine

Although they are ancient creatures, horseshoe crabs are contributing to the future of medicine. Their unusual characteristics make them ideal for many kinds of research. And scientists are still exploring new uses for horseshoe crab blood.

Ten Eyes and a Nobel Prize

The *Limulus polyphemus* was named for Polyphemos—a Cyclops, or one-eyed giant, in Greek mythology. We now know that the horseshoe crab actually has ten eyes. These include a large **compound eye** on either side of its shell, two small **simple eyes** in the center, five light-sensing organs under its shell, and cells in its tail that react to light.

For years scientists wondered why a simple

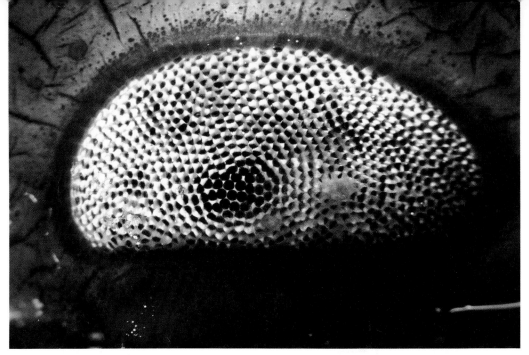

The horseshoe crab's compound eyes contain 1,000 receptors—organs that receive light. Each one registers what it sees as a shade of gray. When put together, these 1,000 dots of varying shades of gray make the image that the crab sees.

animal that spends most of its time on the bottom of the ocean would need so many eyes. They became even more interested when they discovered that the design of the horseshoe crab's compound eyes makes it ideal for studying vision.

In 1926, H. Keffer Hartline went to the Marine Biological Laboratory in Woods Hole, Massachusetts. He wanted to study the basics of sight, and most animals' eyes were too small and complex for this purpose. *Limulus polyphemus* turned out to be an ideal choice. The major parts of the horseshoe crab's eye are the largest of any known animal. They are 100 times the size of a human's. Being able to experiment on such a large eye helped Dr. Hartline learn more about eyesight. For his work, he received a Nobel Prize in 1967.

Years later, Robert B. Barlow, Jr., a student of Hartline's, found that the crab's brain has a **biological clock**, or internal timer, that sends signals to its eyes at night. These signals are like the timer that turns house lights on after dark. They tell the eyes to become up to one million times more sensitive to light. The daily changes in the crab's sensitivity to light assure that the crab sees extremely well in the dark. This unusual ability, says Dr. Barlow, means that the horseshoe crab's underwater world may seem nearly as bright at night as it does during the day.

Studies on horseshoe crab eyes have helped scientists understand how the human eye sees lines,

borders, and contrasts. They have also taught researchers more about human eye diseases.

As it turns out, the "one-eyed giant" can actually
see quite well. In fact, scientists now know that the
horseshoe crab's vision plays a vital role in helping it
find mates.

A Sludgy Surprise

One day in 1955, Dr. Frederick B. Bang of the Marine
Biological Laboratory in Woods Hole, Massachusetts, looked down at the horseshoe crab he had been
studying. He was in the middle of an experiment on
blood flow. But something had happened. The crab's
blood had clotted, or thickened, becoming a sludgy
mess. It would now be useless for his research. Fortunately, he became curious. After some study, he
discovered that the clotting was due to a simple kind
of defense system.

Horseshoe crab blood has a special protective
quality. When the crab's shell is damaged, its blood
forms a jellylike plug that seals off the wound. This

46

prevents **bacteria**, or germs, from entering the rest of the crab's body, where they could do more harm. This protective reaction probably has helped the crab survive in shallow water where there are lots of bacteria. Dr. Bang's discovery opened up new interest in horseshoe crabs.

Scientists realized they could use horseshoe crab blood as a sort of bacteria detector. After some research they found that special cells in the crab's blood could detect not only live bacteria, but also **endotoxins**, chemical poisons given off by some bacteria. If a fluid containing endotoxins is injected into a person's bloodstream, it can cause high fever, shock, even death. In the past, the only way to tell whether a solution contained endotoxins was to inject it into a live rabbit. If the rabbit didn't get a fever, scientists assumed the solution was safe. This test took a long time and was not very sensitive.

Now, a processed form of horseshoe crab blood is used to detect endotoxins in medical fluids. If the fluid being tested contains endotoxins, a substance

Fluids to be tested are put in tubes containing processed horseshoe crab blood. The fluid in the tube that is being held upside down has gelled, indicating it contains endotoxins.

in the horseshoe crab blood makes it gel. Scientists then know for sure that the fluid has been contaminated and should not be used. The Food and Drug Administration (FDA) requires that every injectable drug and solution made in the United States be tested this way to make sure it is pure.

The test can also be used on blood and other body fluids to see if they contain bacteria or endotoxins. If they do, it usually means the patient has an infection or disease. Finding an infection quickly can sometimes mean the difference between life and death.

In the same way, it is important to be sure that blood used for transfusions be pure. In a transfusion, the blood of one person is put into the body of another person. Transfusions are given to replace blood lost during surgery or through an injury. The test using horseshoe crab blood can help make sure that the blood used for transfusions is safe.

New Uses for an Old Animal

Scientists are working on other medical uses for horseshoe crabs. One product being developed is a test that measures the amount of Vitamin B-12 in a person's blood. This test is especially important for newborn babies and older people, who need Vitamin B-12 to avoid serious illnesses.

Horseshoe crab blood is also being used in cancer research. The blood seems to kill abnormal cells such as those found in cancer. Further research may lead to new products for cancer testing and treatment.

Chitin, the substance in horseshoe crab shells, also has interesting properties. Chitin can be broken down into fibers, or threads. When made into bandages, chitin forms a mat of protection over a wound. Skin grows better and wounds heal faster when covered by these special bandages. When spun into a thread, chitin can also be used for sutures—the material used for stitching up cuts or surgical incisions.

Fortunately, the scientists involved in the production of these products understand the importance of preserving the horseshoe crab population. Rather than kill horseshoe crabs for chitin, they use the shucked shells of blue crabs and shrimp. Horseshoe crabs are reserved for research.

Because of their important contributions to modern medicine, horseshoe crabs are considered extremely valuable. These age-old creatures, nearly wiped out by overharvesting, now must be carefully protected.

An Investment in the Future

Scientists and others have been getting the word out about how interesting and important horseshoe crabs are. The first Horseshoe Crab Festival was held on May 31, 1991, in Wildwood Crest, New Jersey. It drew scientists from all over the world and gave ordinary people a chance to learn more about the fascinating horseshoe crab. The festival featured horseshoe crab T-shirts, a puppet show, a 40-foot-long (12.1 meters) sand sculpture of a horseshoe crab, horseshoe crab-shaped hats, and a horseshoe crab king and queen.

The highlight of the festival was the horseshoe crab race. Participants chose their crabs from a tank and then took them down to the starting line, a mark on the beach facing the ocean. At the signal, the crabs were released and they "raced" (at horseshoe crab speed, of course) into the water and to freedom.

Built to Last

Of all the remarkable qualities of the horseshoe crab, perhaps the most remarkable is its ability to survive. This extraordinary creature can live under many different conditions. It can live in areas where the

The first annual Horseshoe Crab Festival featured a race. The competition was intense as the participants prepared their crabs for the "run" to the ocean.

water is near-freezing (Maine) or where it is very warm (Florida). It can live in water with a salt content as low as 8 percent or as high as 36 percent. Horseshoe crabs have been known to survive for a month without food. Some have even lived after being hit by a boat propeller or after suffering a bullet wound.

Horseshoe crabs have survived for millions of years on their own. Now it's up to people to see that they continue to be around for a long time to come.

Sources of Information about the Horseshoe Crab

Write to or visit:

National Aquarium in Baltimore
Pier 3, 501 East Pratt Street
Baltimore, MD 21233
(301) 576-3800

To Adopt a Crab:

People who are interested in helping the horseshoe crab can participate in the Adopt-a-Crab program sponsored by Finn-Tech, a company that bleeds horseshoe crabs for research purposes. For a fee of $10 (which goes toward research on the horseshoe crab), the participant gets a certificate that contains the identification number and release information for an individual tagged crab. If that crab is later found, the person receives information about the crab's location and condition. Write to Finn-Tech Industries, Inc., 7 Bay Avenue/Dias Creek, Cape May Court House, NJ 08210.

Sources of live* or preserved horseshoe crabs:

Carolina Biological Supply Company
P.O. Box 1059
Burlington, NC 27215
(919) 226-6000

Connecticut Valley Biological
82 Valley Road
P.O. Box 326
Southampton, MA 01073
(413) 527-4030

*Horseshoe crabs require special living conditions and are not
suitable as pets.

Glossary

antennae (an-TEN-ee)—a pair of feelers on the head of an animal such as a lobster or crab

arthropods (AR-throw-pods)—animals that have jointed legs, a body divided into two or more parts, and a skeleton on the outside of its body; all arthropods lack a backbone; horseshoe crabs are members of this group

bacteria (back-TEER-ee-a)—creatures made up of only one cell; they are too small to be seen without a microscope; some bacteria cause disease while others cause milk to sour or are used to help ripen cheese

biological clock—an internal timing system in a living organism that causes cycles of behaviors

chitin (KITE-in)—a protein material similar to fingernails that provides a protective covering for the horseshoe crab; also used for making bandages and sutures that help wounds heal faster

compound eye—an eye that consists of many visual units, each having its own lens; messages received from the different units together produce a large field of view that is not sharp in detail; insects and crustaceans have compound eyes

continental shelf—the part of the sea floor that gradually descends from the coastline to depths of about 600 feet (182 meters); from there, the bottom drops down sharply, forming the continental slope to the great depths of the ocean

embryo (EM-bree-oh)—an animal in its first stage of growth, while it is in the egg or in the mother's body

endangered—an animal or plant having a population so low that it is in danger of dying out

endotoxins—poisons released when bacteria die or break apart; if endotoxins enter the bloodstream, fever, shock, or even death can result

evolution(ary) (ev-a-LOO-shun-air-ee)—the theory that plants and animals have slowly developed, or changed, from earlier forms of life over time

exoskeleton (EHKS-oh-SKEHL-uh-tuhn)—the hard skin or shell on many boneless animals, such as insects, crabs, and spiders

extinct (ehk-STINGT)—no longer living anywhere on earth; many plant and animal species have become extinct

fertilize (FURT-il-eyes)—to bring a male sperm cell to a female egg cell during reproduction, causing a new plant or animal to develop

gills—the organs used for breathing by most animals that live in water; gills take oxygen from the water

invertebrate (in-VER-te-brit or in-VER-te-brate)—an animal that has no backbone, such as an insect

larva (LAHR-vuh)—the early form of an animal that looks unlike the parent and that must change before becoming an adult

Limulus polyphemus **(LIM-you-luss polly-FEE-muss)**—the name scientists have given the horseshoe crab; *Limulus* means "looking sideways" (a reference to the crab's compound eyes); *Polyphemus* was the name of a giant Cyclops in Greek mythology who had one eye in the middle of his head; the crab's simple eyes in the center of its body reminded scientists of a Cyclops

living fossil—a *fossil* is the hardened remains or print of a plant or animal that existed many years ago; *living fossil* is the name that people use to describe an animal that has hardly changed over millions of years

molt—to shed fur, feathers, or a shell before they are replaced with new growth

predator (PREHD-uh-tuhr)—an animal that hunts other animals for food

simple eye—an eye that has a single lens; simple eyes can be as small as the horseshoe crab's or as large as the whale's

species (SPEE-shees)—a group of plants or animals that share similar features; usually, only animals of the same species can mate and produce young

sperm—the cells produced by the male sex organs; it is these cells that are capable of fertilizing the eggs of the female

trilobite (TRI-le-bite)—an arthropod that lived in the sea millions of years ago; many fossils of trilobites have been found

Index

Nancy Day first became interested in horseshoe crabs when she worked for a company that processes horseshoe crab blood. Part of her job was explaining the horseshoe crab's medical uses to employees, customers, and members of the community. She now lives in West Chester, Pennsylvania, with her husband and son. They frequently vacation on the Delaware shore, happily sharing the beach with the horseshoe crabs.

Ms. Day has published numerous articles for *Cobblestone, Dolphin Log, Odyssey, Faces,* and several other magazines. This is her first book for Dillon Press.